GREEN GIANTS

Twelve of the Earth's Tallest Trees

By Sneed B. Collard III

NORTHWORD
PRESS, INC

Minocqua, Wisconsin

Dedicated to Dr. A.C. Carder,
for devoting your life to
the magic of our silent neighbors.

Edited by Greg Linder
Designed by Patricia Bickner Linder

Published by: NorthWord Press, Inc.
            P.O. Box 1360
            Minocqua, WI 54548

For a free catalog describing NorthWord's line of nature books and gifts, call 1-800-336-5666.

Library of Congress Cataloging-in-Publication Data

Collard, Sneed B.
        Green giants / by Sneed Collard.
            p. cm.
        Includes bibliographical references.
        Summary: Describes twelve of the world's tallest trees, such as the redwood, mountain ash, kauri, and Douglas fir.
            ISBN 1-55971-222-8 : $9.95
            1. Trees—Juvenile literature. [1. Trees.] I. Title.
        QK475.8.C654 1994
        582.16—dc20   93–15936
                                                          CIP
                                                          AC

Printed in Singapore

TABLE OF CONTENTS

About Trees

*Beauty. Shade. Food. Paper.
Houses. Fuel. Oxygen. Water.
Wildlife. Rubber. Soil. Safety.
Clothing. Medicine. Fun . . .*

We depend on trees for so many things that it's hard to imagine living without them. And as more and more people are born, we will need trees more than ever.

Trees give us foods like apples and oranges. They provide us with fuel for heating and cooking. They give us the material to make thousands of things we use every day, including houses. By taking in carbon dioxide and releasing oxygen into the atmosphere, trees also help solve our worst environmental problems—like global warming and air pollution.

But trees are in trouble. Even though people plant billions of trees each year, our planting isn't keeping up with the number of trees we use. We are cutting down and burning the world's forests at an alarming rate. As you read this book, think about all the ways that trees make our lives better. On the last page, you'll find a list of things you can do to help make sure that trees and forests are always part of our world.

3

About Tall Trees

Trees grow in all shapes and sizes. Some trees are fat, spreading their limbs over wide areas. Others are so tiny they could get lost in your bedroom. But this book isn't about just *any* trees. This book is only about trees that are giants—trees that grow very, very, VERY tall.

In this book, you'll learn about every single one of the giant trees you see on these two pages. To find out about them, you'll travel to California, Australia,

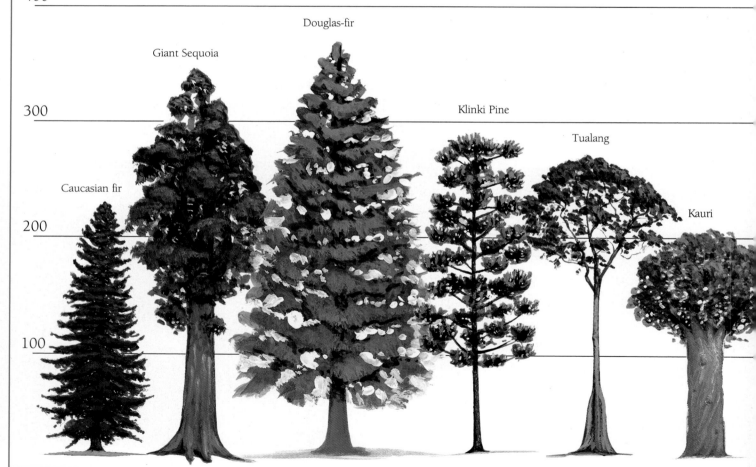

Height in feet

400

300

200

100

Caucasian fir

Giant Sequoia

Douglas-fir

Klinki Pine

Tualang

Kauri

Africa, New Guinea, and many more places. You'll find out how tall the trees grow and where they live. You'll learn which animals depend on the trees, and why each tree is important to people. You'll also realize just how old some of the world's tallest trees are. Many giant trees have spent hundreds of years getting so big. When we cut down a green giant, we have to wait a long time before another tree gets just as big.

You won't find every tall tree in this book. Even a book called *Green Giants* has space for only a few of the world's giants. But when you're finished reading, I hope you're excited about tall trees. Even if you never get to visit the very tallest of trees, keep a special place in your heart for the green giants of our world.

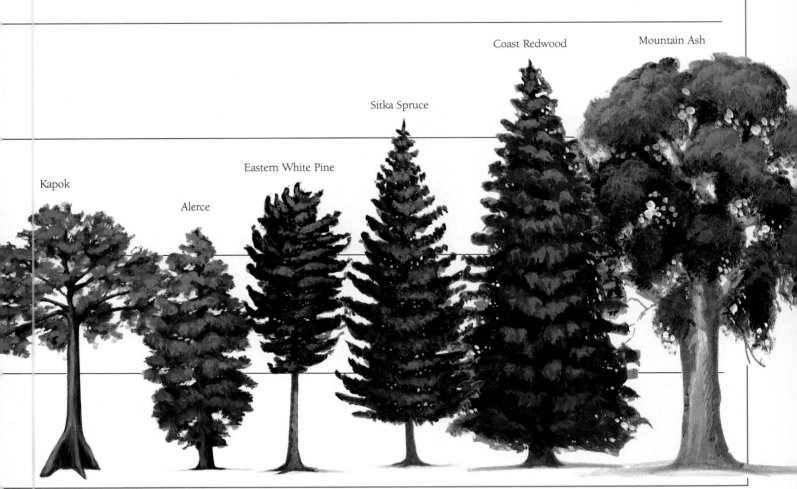

Coast Redwood

FAST FACTS

▶ **Scientific Name . . .**
Sequoia sempervirens
(SE-KWOY-UH SEM-PER-VEER-ENS)
▶ **Kind of Tree . . .**
Conifer
▶ **Tallest Ever Measured . . .**
380 Feet
▶ **Widest Trunk Diameter . . .**
33 Feet
▶ **Oldest . . .**
2,000 Years

Among all of the tall trees in the world, coast redwoods are the tallest. Redwoods belong to a large group of trees called **conifers**. The seeds of these trees grow in cones, such as pine cones. Conifers are often called **softwoods** because their wood is soft and easy to shape.

DAVID HARVEY/NATIONAL
GEOGRAPHIC SOCIETY

LINDA MAUZY

A redwood starts life as a tiny seed just three times as big as the head of a pin. If it sprouts in good soil and gets enough water and sunlight, a young tree might grow two to six feet per year.

Redwood bark can be over a foot thick. The bark is like a skin that protects the tree from diseases and fire. Scientists found one redwood that had survived nine major forest fires during the last 1,000 years.

A giant redwood's roots are shallow, but they can spread out for over an acre—about the size of a football field.

Fifteen kinds of salamanders live in redwood forests. Black bears, deer, mountain lions, and Roosevelt elk wander among these giant trees, too.

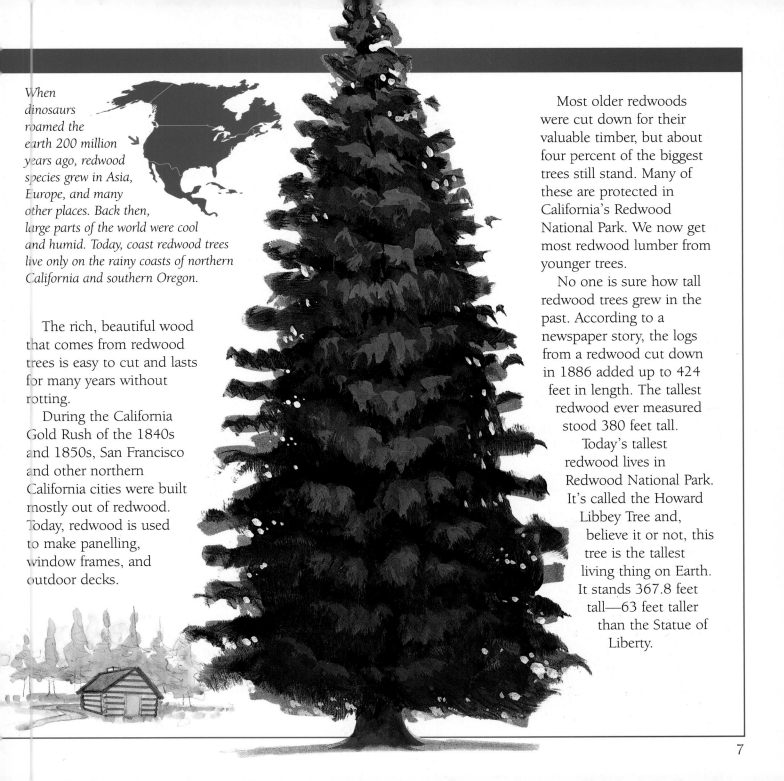

When dinosaurs roamed the earth 200 million years ago, redwood species grew in Asia, Europe, and many other places. Back then, large parts of the world were cool and humid. Today, coast redwood trees live only on the rainy coasts of northern California and southern Oregon.

The rich, beautiful wood that comes from redwood trees is easy to cut and lasts for many years without rotting.

During the California Gold Rush of the 1840s and 1850s, San Francisco and other northern California cities were built mostly out of redwood. Today, redwood is used to make panelling, window frames, and outdoor decks.

Most older redwoods were cut down for their valuable timber, but about four percent of the biggest trees still stand. Many of these are protected in California's Redwood National Park. We now get most redwood lumber from younger trees.

No one is sure how tall redwood trees grew in the past. According to a newspaper story, the logs from a redwood cut down in 1886 added up to 424 feet in length. The tallest redwood ever measured stood 380 feet tall.

Today's tallest redwood lives in Redwood National Park. It's called the Howard Libbey Tree and, believe it or not, this tree is the tallest living thing on Earth. It stands 367.8 feet tall—63 feet taller than the Statue of Liberty.

Mountain Ash

The mountain ash is one of over 500 different kinds of trees that are called eucalyptus trees, or eucalypts. Before Europeans started logging in Australia, eucalypts were probably the tallest trees in the world—even taller than coast redwoods. More than a dozen species of eucalypts now reach over 200 feet high, and the mountain ash is the tallest of these tall trees.

FAST FACTS

▶ **Scientific Name . . .**
Eucalyptus regnans
(YOU-KA-LIP-TUS REG-NANZ)
▶ **Kind of Tree . . .**
Flowering Broad-leaved
▶ **Tallest Ever Measured . . .**
435 Feet
▶ **Widest Trunk Diameter . . .**
35 Feet
▶ **Oldest . . .**
500 Years

JOYCE PHOTOGRAPHICS/PHOTO RESEARCHERS

Eucalypt seeds grow in flowers instead of cones. Flowering trees are called **hardwoods**, because their wood is often tough and hard. Flowering trees are also called **broad-leaved trees**, because they have large, flat leaves.

Eucalypts grow in many different conditions. Some flourish in deserts that get less than ten inches of rain per year. But the mountain ash needs plenty of water and cool temperatures. It grows best in the deep, moist soils of mountain valleys.

Parrots, kingfishers, and kangaroos live in eucalypt forests. One of Australia's most famous animals—the koala—eats nothing but the leaves of eucalyptus trees.

A few species of eucalypts grow in Papua New Guinea, and one species lives in the Philippines. But most eucalypts come from Australia. The mountain ash is native only to Australia's southeast corner.

The bark of many eucalyptus trees peels off in long strips. Australia's natives, called aborigines, used this bark to make clothing and canoes.

The tallest tree ever discovered was an Australian mountain ash. When it fell, it formed a natural bridge across a canyon. In 1872, a forest inspector named William Ferguson measured the tree and found that it was 435 long and 18 feet wide, even though the top of the tree had broken off. Ferguson guessed that the tree *originally* stood more than 500 feet high—almost as tall as the Washington Monument.

People have planted eucalypts in many countries. In fact, these trees are the most common source of hardwood lumber in the world. People also burn them for fuel and use them to make paper, perfume, and even cough drops. Look around—chances are, someone has planted a eucalypt near you.

Kauri

Many wonderful kinds of trees grow in New Zealand, but the great kauri (COW-REE) is by far the largest. Like the coast redwood, the kauri is a conifer that grows seeds in its cones.

FAST FACTS

▶ **Scientific Name . . .**
Agathis australis
(AG-UH-THIS AW-STRAL-IS)

▶ **Kind of Tree . . .**
Conifer

▶ **Tallest Ever Measured . . .**
Over 200 Feet

▶ **Widest Trunk Diameter . . .**
24 Feet

▶ **Oldest . . .**
More than 2,000 Years

JOHN SHAW

NOW'S MY CHANCE

New Zealand forests—and many other forests—are very dark places. That's because the treetops form a **canopy** above, which blocks out most of the sunlight.

The shade of the canopy makes it hard for kauri seeds to start growing. To get bigger, young kauris need an opening in the canopy that lets the sunlight through. Openings can happen as a result of forest fires. They're also created when big trees fall or are cut down. When a kauri is given some light, it shoots up quickly. By the time it's an adult, it towers way above the other trees in the forest.

New Zealand's famous kiwi bird lives in kauri forests. So do bats, giant snails and wetas, which are big insects related to crickets.

The kauri lives only at the northern tip of New Zealand's North Island, but over a dozen of the kauri's relatives are found in nearby Australia and Southeast Asia.

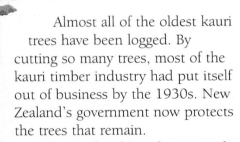

Kauris may live to be more than 2,000 years old. **Dendrologists**—scientists who study trees—usually determine a tree's age by counting the growth rings in the tree's trunk. But the centers of many old kauris have rotted away, so the scientists have to guess how old the trees are.

New Zealand's Maori people carved huge canoes out of kauri trees. When Europeans arrived in New Zealand in the 1800s, they used the straight, strong kauri wood to build sailing ships. Kauri soon earned a reputation as the world's best ship-building wood.

Almost all of the oldest kauri trees have been logged. By cutting so many trees, most of the kauri timber industry had put itself out of business by the 1930s. New Zealand's government now protects the trees that remain.

Today's tallest living kauri stands 185 feet high, but experts are sure that kauris have grown more than 200 feet tall in the past. Searching for big kauri trees has become a hobby for some New Zealanders. Someday a lucky New Zealander may find a living kauri that's 200 feet tall.

Tualang

Like eucalyptus trees, the tualang (TOO-UH-LONG) is a flowering broad-leaved tree. In the tropical rain forest where the tualang is found, over 800 tree species may live close together. This is about twice the number of tree species you'll find in all of temperate North America. But the tualang towers above most of its tropical neighbors.

FAST FACTS

▶ **Scientific Name . . .**
Koompassia excelsa
(KOOM-PA-SEE-UH EX-SEL-SUH)

▶ **Kind of Tree . . .**
Flowering Broad-leaved

▶ **Tallest Ever Measured . . .**
275 Feet

▶ **Widest Trunk Diameter . . .**
10 Feet

▶ **Oldest . . .**
300 Years

The Malaysian rain forest is one of the most amazing places on Earth. Tigers, elephants, rhinos, and birds called hornbills live there. In the morning, the haunting hoots of gibbons, the smallest members of the ape family, echo through the dark, lush forest. Here, tualangs must grow tall to reach the sunlight.

Honeybees love to nest in tualang trees, and one tree may hold as many as a dozen beehives. Native Malaysians climb up tualang trees to get the honey. It's dangerous work, but a team of bee-hunters can earn hundreds of dollars from the honey of a single tualang.

The tualang—like many large rain forest trees—grows enormous **buttresses** at the bottom of its trunk. People often think these thickened bases help hold the trees up, but buttressed trees seem to fall down just as often as trees without them.

KEN RUBELI/PICTURE LIBRARY SDN. BHD.

14

The Sitka spruce thrives in cool, coastal climates. Its native range stretches from northern California to southern Alaska, but it really becomes a green giant in Washington and British Columbia. It often grows alongside western hemlock, Douglas-fir, and coast redwood trees.

CULVER PICTURES

During the First and Second World Wars, airplanes were made from Sitka spruce. The sturdy spruce wings of the *Spirit of St. Louis* carried aviator Charles Lindbergh on his famous first flight across the Atlantic Ocean.

Sitka spruce was used to build a water plane called the Spruce Goose. Billionaire Howard Hughes spent $40 million to build the water plane. Unfortunately, the goose laid an egg—it flew just once, and it never climbed more than 70 feet into the air.

Because its wood is so useful, Sitka spruce has been heavily logged in recent years. Most Sitkas are cut for lumber and wood pulp. Pulp is used to make hundreds of products, including paper, plastics, tooth-paste, clothing, explosives, salad dressing, and rocket fuel.

Many Sitka spruce live in the Tongass National Forest of Alaska. It is one of North America's largest temperate-zone rain forests. Over 5.4 million acres of the Tongass are now protected—an area half the size of the state of Rhode Island.

The tallest Sitka spruce ever measured is called the Carmanah Giant. It soars 312 feet into the sky, and it is Canada's tallest tree. The Carmanah Giant's home is a lush valley on the west coast of Vancouver Island.

19

Caucasian Fir

FAST FACTS

▶ **Scientific Name . . .**
Abies nordmanianna
(A-BEEZ NORD-MAN-E-AH-NA)
▶ **Kind of Tree . . .**
Conifer
▶ **Tallest Ever Measured . . .**
229.5 Feet
▶ **Widest Trunk Diameter . . .**
9 Feet
▶ **Oldest . . .**
700 Years

Fir trees are among the world's loveliest and tallest trees. About 50 kinds of firs live in the cooler climates of the northern hemisphere.

SUE THOMAS/HOYT ARBORETUM

Caucasian firs grow best in deep mountain valleys, where the air is humid. They thrive in deep, rich soil, and they send their roots far into the earth. Because they're anchored so firmly, Caucasian firs are rarely blown over by the wind.

Like many other fir trees, the Caucasian fir provides soft, high-quality lumber. The wood is used to construct buildings and for general carpentry. The tree's thin, gray bark is often made into turpentine, which is used as a paint thinner.

The Caucasian fir has a small native range in western Asia, but it grows especially well in Europe. Many Europeans plant these trees in their gardens, and the Caucasian fir is a favorite Christmas tree in Denmark.

The Caucasian fir gets its name from its home in the Caucasus Mountains. These mountains rise up near the Black Sea in the country of Georgia— a part of the former Soviet Union. The Caucasian fir is also found in nearby Turkey.

German scientists have discovered that the Caucasian fir can withstand some kinds of air pollution. In the future, the tree may be used to replant forests that were killed by **acid rain**. Acid rain is caused when sulfur dioxide and nitrogen oxides are released into the air by cars, factories, volcanoes, and other sources. When the chemicals mix with rain, they harm trees, fish, and aquatic wildlife. Acid rain has killed or damaged millions of trees in Europe and North America.

Caucasian fir forests cover over five million acres of mountains in the country of Georgia. The fir often grows near spruce and beech trees, but in remote valleys of Georgia and Turkey, pure stands of tall Caucasian firs sway gently in the breeze.

The Caucasian fir is the tallest of all trees found in western Asia or Europe. One Caucasian fir stood 229.5 feet tall. A giant tree like that could provide shade for the Egyptian pyramids.

SUE THOMAS/HOYT ARBORETUM

Klinki Pine

The klinki pine is the tallest tree that lives in tropical rain forests. It belongs to the same family of trees as New Zealand's kauri tree. These trees are often called pines, but they're not in the same family as North American pine trees.

FAST FACTS

- **Scientific Name . . .**
  Araucaria hunsteinii
  (AR-UH-CARE-E-UH HUN-STEN-EYE)
- **Kind of Tree . . .**
  Conifer
- **Tallest Ever Measured . . .**
  292 Feet
- **Widest Trunk Diameter . . .**
  6.5 Feet
- **Oldest . . .**
  700 Years

ALAN WATSON/FOREST LIGHT

The klinki pine grows on high mountain slopes and in lowland valleys. It is one of the few conifers that thrives in Papua New Guinea's lowland rain forest. Most lowland rain forest trees are flowering broad-leaved trees.

Under the dense shade of broad-leaved trees, young klinki pines often can't get enough sunlight to grow. Like kauris, klinki pines need an opening in the forest canopy to get started.

ALAN WATSON/FOREST LIGHT

22

The klinki pine's ancestors once grew in many parts of the earth. Today, the klinki's relatives are found in Australia, in South America, and on islands of the Pacific Ocean. The klinki pine, though, grows only in eastern Papua New Guinea.

When they do grow, adult klinkis tower high above the rest of the forest. Trees that grow much taller than the trees around them are called **emergent trees**. The kauri and the tualang are also emergent trees.

One animal that especially likes klinki pines is the sulphur-crested cockatoo. Cockatoos land in the treetops and feast on klinki pine cones. These birds might devour half of the tree's pine cones each year.

Like the tribes of Malaysia, native New Guineans depend on their forests for food, fire-wood, and many other things. They also make drums out of klinki pine wood. The tree's sap is a natural glue that holds the top of each drum in place.

The wood from klinki pine is used to make furniture, boats, plywood, beekeepers' hives, and chopsticks. Klinki and one of its close relatives are the most important timber trees in New Guinea.

Klinki pine is grown on plantations in New Guinea. Other countries, such as Malaysia, have begun to plant the klinki pine. Someday it may be an important timber tree for many tropical countries.

23

Kapok

FAST FACTS

The kapok or silk cotton tree is one of the world's tallest and most famous tropical trees. The kapok is also one of the few tropical trees that is **cosmopolitan**. Cosmopolitan plants and animals are those that live in many parts of the world.

- ▶ **Scientific Name . . .**
  Ceiba pentandra
  (SEE-BUH PEN-TAN-DRUH)
- ▶ **Kind of Tree . . .**
  Flowering Broad-leaved Tree
- ▶ **Tallest Ever Measured . . .**
  246 Feet
- ▶ **Widest Trunk Diameter . . .**
  7.8 Feet
- ▶ **Oldest . . .**
  250 Years

ALAN WATSON/FOREST LIGHT

Bats, hummingbirds, and opossums live on or near kapok trees. In Peru, over a dozen species of mammals feed on the nectar of kapok flowers. The animals get a free meal, but they also pollinate the tree's flowers, which helps more kapok trees grow. From Mexico to Brazil, kapok trees provide nesting sites for giant harpy eagles—the world's most powerful birds of prey.

Kapok seed pods are filled with light, waterproof fibers that look and feel like cotton. These fibers make the seed pods float and help the tree spread to many places.

People use kapok fibers for stuffing pillows, mattresses, and life preservers. After the kapok seeds have been separated from the fibers, the seeds are turned into soap and cooking oil and are sometimes fed to cattle. In Tanzania, the tree's bark is boiled into a tea that helps stop heart pain.

ROBERT AND LINDA MITCHELL

Finding Green Giants

You might be asking yourself, "How does someone find big trees?" Finding them is not as easy as you might think. Since many giant trees live deep within forests, locating them can be difficult. Even when you *do* find one, measuring it is a challenge. Very precise tools are needed—and a lot of patience.

But this doesn't stop people all over the world from looking for big trees. In the U.S., a group called American Forests keeps track of the biggest examples of each tree species. Trees are judged not only by their height, but by the width of their trunks and their crowns. American Forests publishes the current "tree champions" in a booklet called the *National Register of Big Trees*. Over 800 recordholding trees are listed in the register. To find out how to get a copy, write to:

American Forests
National Register of Big Trees
P.O. Box 2000
Washington, DC   20013

Be sure to ask for information about how you can find big trees and how you can help our forests. And keep your eyes on the sky—maybe you'll be the next famous discoverer of a green giant!

RICH BUZZELLI/TOM STACK AND ASSOCIATES

31

Protecting Our Trees

Many of our planet's forests have been destroyed, but you can help protect the millions of green treasures that remain. Just reading this book helps. If you tell your friends what you have learned, you can help everyone understand more about trees, forests, and our environment. Here are more things you can do:

1) Take your own bag with you when you go shopping. Then you won't need a bag from the store. Bags are usually made from trees, so the fewer bags we use, the fewer trees we have to cut down.
2) Plant a tree. Be sure to pick a species that grows naturally in your area. A native tree is more likely to survive than a tree that comes from somewhere else. It will also provide better food and shelter for local wildlife.
3) Recycle newspapers, old homework, and any other paper that you don't need.
4) Write to a group that protects trees or forests. Ask them for information on their work and how you can help. Here are a few important groups to get you started:

Rainforest Action Network
450 Sansome St., Suite 700
San Francisco, CA 94111
(Works to protect rain forests
and rain forest peoples)

Ancient Forests International
P.O. Box 1850
Redway, CA 95560
(Works to protect alerces and other trees
of South America)

Save-the-Redwoods League
114 Sansome St., Room 605
San Francisco, CA 94104
(Works to protect coast redwoods
and giant sequoias)

The Wilderness Society
900 Seventeenth St. NW
Washington, D.C. 20006-2596
(Works on forest protection and other
environmental issues)

Part of the cost of this book is donated to groups that plant and protect trees.